The DICTIONARY of DIFFICULT WORDS

Frances Lincoln
Children's Books

WELCOME, WORDSMITHS!

Words are wonderful! Without words, we wouldn't be able to share all our ideas with the people around us. That's why we've put together a dictionary that will take you on a journey through some of the most brilliant and surprising words in the English language.

WHAT IS A DICTIONARY?

A dictionary is a collection of words and their meanings. Sometimes dictionaries are books you can hold, like this book, and sometimes they're digital. Dictionaries are written by **LEXICOGRAPHERS** (pages 51 and 53). Lexicographers study how people use language, and then write down what they learn in dictionaries.

You'll find many different types of words in this dictionary. The longest words are **SPAGHETTIFICATION** (pages 80-81) and **TRISKAIDEKAPHOBIA** (page 84), and the shortest word is **X** (page 99). Some of the words are used all the time like **OMINOUS** (page 63), while others are so rare that you might only find them in an old book, like **SESQUIPEDALIAN** (page 79). Some words are fun to say like **HURDY-GURDY** (pages 36-37), and others have definitions that describe beautiful things in the world like **MOONBOW** (page 56).

RAVE

SALUBRIOUS

darkle

GENERAL STORE
WORDS
new & SECOND-HAND
bibliophile
TURN

X-RAY

GERRY

cacophony

HIRS

QUIXOTIC

imagineer

HOW TO READ THIS BOOK

There is no right way to read this book. Here are just a few ideas, but feel free to come up with your own favorite way of reading *The Dictionary of Difficult Words*.

1. You can read it straight through from A to Z.
2. You can read it backward from Z to A.
3. You can read one letter of the alphabet at a time.
4. You can read it out loud with loved ones.
5. You can read it silently by yourself.
6. You can look at the pictures and not read the words.
7. You can open up to a random page, close your eyes, put your finger down, and then read what you're pointing at.
8. You can read a word out loud and then let someone guess what the definition is.
9. You can read it in the dark with a flashlight.
10. You can read it to learn new things, or you can read it just for fun.

Look out for the clouds around some of our favorite definitions. You can find extra information about the word in a cloud, along with a big illustration, on a nearby page.

PARTS OF SPEECH

A word's part of speech gives you information about how it's used in a sentence. The definitions in this book have one of these three parts of speech:

adjective
An adjective is a word used to describe nouns and to give extra information about someone or something. *Big*, *gray*, and *smart* are all adjectives.

HOT

LOOK

ME

JUMP

smart

BiG

HOW TO WORK OUT WHAT A WORD MEANS

Sometimes we can find clues about a word's meaning if we look at how it's spelled.

If a word ends with *-ology*, it's about something you study (see **CRYPTOZOOLOGY** on page 16), and if a word ends with *-ologist*, it's about the people who study that thing (see **ICHTHYOLOGIST** on page 39).

If a word ends in *-phile*, it's about a person who loves something (see **BIBLIOPHILE** on page 11).

If a word ends in *-ous*, it's probably an adjective (see **LUMINOUS** on page 52).

If a word has *-graph* in it, it's often about writing (see **ORTHOGRAPHY** on page 64).

If a word ends in *-ism*, it's probably a noun (see **ANACHRONISM** on page 8).

HOW TO WORK OUT HOW TO SAY A WORD

If you're a big reader, you often learn new words from books. You might know a word's meaning, but when it comes to saying it, you have no idea how to pronounce it. This happens to people of all ages, so you're not alone. Many of the words in this book are hard to say. English rules can be extremely confusing. For instance, the letter X can sometimes be pronounced like Z, and *-ough* can be said in many different ways in English, like in the words *cough*, *dough*, and *through*. Luckily, there is a handy pronunciation guide underneath each word to help you work out how to say it.

Turn the page to start your journey of discovery!

ABECEDARIAN

[ey-bee-see-**dair**-ee-*uhn*] · *noun*

An abecedarian is someone who is learning the alphabet or who is a beginner in any subject.

ABSQUATULATE

[ab-**skwoch**-*uh*-leyt] · *verb*

When someone absquatulates, they leave a place very

quickly and without warning. People use this word when they want to be funny.

AESTHETIC

[es-**thet**-ik] · *noun*

When someone uses the word aesthetic, they are talking about what makes something

beautiful to them. People often use this word when they're talking about art.

AFFABLE

[**af**-*uh*-buhl] · *adjective*

Someone who is affable is friendly and fun to talk to.

AILUROPHILE

[ahy-**loor**-*uh*-fahyl] · *noun*

An ailurophile is someone who loves cats.

ALIENATE

[**ey**-lee-*uh*-neyt] · *verb*

If you alienate someone, you make them feel sad and like they are all alone.

ALOOF

[*uh*-loof] · *adjective*

When someone is aloof, they are not very friendly or easy to talk to.

AMBIDEXTROUS

[am-bi-**dek**-struhs] · *adjective*

When someone is ambidextrous, they can use both their right and left hands to write or draw.

AMBIVALENT

[am-**biv**-*uh*-luhnt] · *adjective*

When you are ambivalent about something, you feel two very different ways about it at the same time.

ANACHRONISM

[uh-**nak**-ruh-niz-uhm] · *noun*

An anachronism is something that doesn't fit into its surroundings because it belongs to a different time or era.

Sometimes things that are old-fashioned are called anachronisms.

ANATHEMA

[uh-**nath**-uh-muh] · *noun*

If something is anathema to someone, they really hate it.

ANTITHESIS

[an-**tith**-uh-sis] · *noun*

The antithesis of something is the opposite of that thing.

ARACHNOPHOBIA

[uh-rak-nuh-**foh**-bee-uh] · *noun*

Arachnophobia is an extreme fear of spiders.

ARBITRARY

[**ahr**-bi-trer-ee] · *adjective*

When a rule is arbitrary, there is no real reason why it is the way it is.

ARCANE

[ahr-**keyn**] · *adjective*

When something is arcane, it is mysterious or difficult to understand.

ARID

[**ar**-id] · *adjective*

If a place is arid, it is very dry and it doesn't rain much there. Deserts have arid climates.

AVUNCULAR

[uh-**vuhng**-kyuh-ler] · *adjective*

Avuncular is a word that describes uncles and people who act like uncles. If someone is avuncular, they are helpful and friendly to people who are younger than them.

ARID

One type of plant that thrives in hot
and arid climates is the cactus.
Cacti are extremely good at collecting
and storing water and can survive for
months and months without rain.

BAILIWICK

[**bey**-luh-wik] · *noun*

Someone's bailiwick is something they know a lot about, or a thing that they are really good at.

BEDAZZLED

[bih-**daz**-uhld] · *adjective*

When you are bedazzled by something, you are so impressed by it that you don't notice the bad things about it.

BEHEMOTH

[bih-**hee**-muhth] · *noun*

A behemoth is a monster or a very large and powerful animal, person, or thing.

BELLWETHER

[**bel**-weth-er] · *noun*

A bellwether is someone who does things in a new way that changes how others think about the world. Often, a bellwether is not aware of the effect that they have on others.

BESPECTACLED

[bih-**spek**-tuh-kuhld] · *adjective*

Someone who is bespectacled is wearing glasses.

BIBLIOPHILE

[**bib**-lee-uh-fahyl] · *noun*

A bibliophile is a person who collects or loves books.

BILDUNGSROMAN

[**bil**-doongz-roh-mahn] · *noun*

A Bildungsroman is a story about someone who is growing up and learning about who they are. This is sometimes called a coming-of-age story.

BIOLUMINESCENT
[bahy-oh-loo-muh-**nes**-uhnt] · *adjective*
When a living thing is bioluminescent, it glows in the dark.

BLATHERSKITE
[**blath**-er-skahyt] · *noun*
A blatherskite is a person who talks a lot, but says things that are meaningless or foolish.

BLITHESOME
[**blahyth**-suhm] · *adjective*
When someone is blithesome, they are full of light-hearted joy. If something is blithesome, it is so wonderful that it can make others happy.

BORBORYGMUS
[bohr-buh-**rig**-muhs] · *noun*
Borborygmus is the rumbling sound that comes from someone's stomach.

BROWBEAT
[**brou**-beet] · *verb*

If you browbeat someone into doing something, you bully them into acting a certain way.

BUGBEAR
[**buhg**-bair] · *noun*
A bugbear is something that makes you feel needlessly scared or annoyed.

BUMBERSHOOT
[**buhm**-ber-shoot] · *noun*
A bumbershoot is an umbrella.

BIOLUMINESCENT

Fireflies are bioluminescent, and this helps them find and recognize one another. Different types of fireflies flash in different patterns and colors. The flash of a firefly can appear as yellow, white, green, or blue.

100

CACHINNATE

[kak-*uh*-neyt] · *verb*

When someone cachinnates, they laugh very loudly.

CACOPHONY

[kuh-kof-*uh*-nee] · *noun*

A cacophony is a mixture of loud and annoying sounds, all happening at the same time.

CANDOR

[kan-der] · *noun*

Candor is being honest and telling the truth, even if it's hard to do.

CANTANKEROUS

[kan-**tang**-ker-*uhs*] · *adjective*

When someone is cantankerous, they want to argue and complain about everything.

CATOPTROMANCY

[ka-**top**-truh-**man**-see] · *noun*

Catoptromancy is when people use mirrors to uncover hidden knowledge. The queen in *Snow White* is practicing catoptromancy when she looks into her mirror and asks *Mirror, mirror, on the wall, who's the fairest one of all?*

CAVORT

[kuh-**vohrt**] · *verb*

When someone cavorts, they dance or jump around with excitement.

CENTENARIAN

[sen-tn-**air**-ee-*uhn*] · *noun*

A centenarian is someone who is 100 years old or older.

CERULEAN

[suh-**roo**-lee-*uhn*] · *noun*

Cerulean is a deep blue color, like a cloudless daytime sky.

CHILIAD

[**kil**-ee-ad] · *noun*

A chiliad is a period of 1,000 years or any group of 1,000 things.

CHIMERA

[kahy-**meer**-*uh*] · *noun*

A chimera is a fire-breathing monster with the head of a lion, the body of a goat, and the tail of a snake.

CIRCUMLOCUTION

[sur-*kuhm*-loh-**kyoo**-shuhn] · *noun*

Circumlocution is when someone uses a lot of words to say something they could have said with very few words.

CLOWDER

[**klou**-der] · *noun*

A clowder is a group of cats.

COCKALORUM

[kok-*uh*-**lohr**-*uhm*] · *noun*

A cockalorum is someone who thinks that they are more important than they actually are.

COGNIZANT

[**kog**-nuh-zuhnt] · *adjective*

When someone is cognizant of something, they are aware of it.

COMPUNCTION

[kuhm-**puhngk**-shuhn] · *noun*

If someone has no compunction about something they've done, they don't feel bad or guilty about it.

CONNIVE

[kuh-**nahyv**] · *verb*

If you connive with someone to do something, you work together to make a secret plan that will benefit both of you.

CRUCIVERBALIST

[kroo-s*uh*-**vur**-b*uh*-list] · *noun*

A cruciverbalist is someone who creates or loves solving crossword puzzles.

CRYPTOZOOLOGY

Are unicorns real? This is a question a cryptozoologist might ask. Unicorns have popped up in the stories and art of various cultures since ancient times. However there is no scientific evidence that these horned creatures exist.

DABSTER

[**dab**-ster] · *noun*

A dabster is someone who is an expert at something.

DARKLE

[**dahr**-kuhl] · *verb*

If something darkles, it becomes less and less light or more and more dark.

DEFENESTRATE

[dee-**fen**-uh-streyt] · *verb*

If you defenestrate something, you throw it out of a window.

DEIPNOSOPHIST

[dahyp-**nos**-uh-fist] · *noun*

A deipnosophist is someone who is very good at having interesting conversations with others while sitting down for a meal.

DEMOGORGON

[dem-uh-**gohr**-guhn] · *noun*

A demogorgon is a mysterious and powerful mythological god or demon.

DENDRIFORM

[**den**-druh-fohrm] · *adjective*

Something that is dendriform is shaped like a tree.

DEVOUR

[dih-**vou**-uhr] · *verb*

If you devour food, you eat it very quickly. If you devour a book, you read it really fast.

DILAPIDATED

[dih-**lap**-i-dey-tid] · *adjective*

When something is dilapidated, it is old and falling apart. People often use this word to talk about buildings.

DISPARATE

[**dis**-per-it] · *adjective*

When things are disparate, they are very clearly different from each other, like chalk and cheese.

DOPPELGÄNGER

[**dop**-*uhl*-gang-er] · *noun*

A doppelgänger is someone who looks exactly like someone else. They might look so much like another person that it's spooky.

DORYPHORE

[**dohr**-*uh*-fohr] · *noun*

A doryphore is someone who is annoying because they like to point out when others make small mistakes.

DRACONIAN

[druh-**koh**-nee-uhn] · *adjective*

When rules or laws are called draconian, they are thought to be cruel or unfair.

DROLL

[drohl] · *adjective*

When something is droll, it is funny in a strange or surprising way.

DRUDGERY

[**druhj**-*uh*-ree] · *noun*

Drudgery is hard work that is very boring, but has to be done.

DUBIOUS

[**doo**-bee-uhs] · *adjective*

When something is dubious, it is doubtful or uncertain.

DUMBFOUNDED

[**duhm**-found-id] · *adjective*

When someone is dumbfounded, they are so surprised by something that they don't know what to do.

DUPLICITY

[doo-**plis**-i-tee] · *noun*

People use the word duplicity when they are talking about misleading or untrustworthy behavior.

DOPPELGÄNGER

In German folklore, your doppelgänger is a supernatural being that looks exactly like you. It's like a ghost, but it appears while someone is still alive. Seeing your own doppelgänger is not a good thing because, according to legend, they appear shortly before someone dies. Usually when people use the word doppelgänger, they're not talking about death. They just mean that someone looks a lot like you.

EARWORM

[eer-wurm] . *noun*

An earworm is a song that keeps on playing over and over in your head, even when you try not to think about it.

EBULLIENT

[ih-**buhl**-*yuhnt*] . *adjective*

Someone who is ebullient is extremely excited or enthusiastic about something.

ECLECTIC

[ih-**klek**-tik] . *adjective*

When a group of things is eclectic, everything that makes up that group comes from different places. If someone has eclectic taste in music, it means they like a lot of different styles of music.

EGGHEAD

[eg-hed] . *noun*

An egghead is someone who is very smart, but not always in ways that are useful for day-to-day life. People sometimes use this word when they don't value someone's knowledge.

EMULATE

[em-*yuh*-leyt] . *verb*

If you emulate someone, you try to be just like them because you think they're great.

ENNUI

[ahn-**wee**] . *noun*

If someone feels ennui, they are bored and tired and have no interest in the things going on around them.

ENUNCIATE

[ih-**nuhn**-see-eyt] . *verb*

When someone enunciates, they say words very clearly and carefully.

EPIGRAM

[ep-i-gram] · *noun*

An epigram is something you say that is quick, clever, and funny. The Irish writer Oscar Wilde is famous for his many epigrams. For example: *When people agree with me I always feel that I must be wrong.*

EQUANIMITY

[ek-wuh-nim-i-tee] · *noun*

Equanimity is being calm and thoughtful, especially in a stressful or difficult situation.

ERGOPHOBIA

[ur-guh-foh-bee-uh] · *noun*

Ergophobia is a fear of work. People use this word when they want to be funny.

ESTIVAL

[es-tuh-vuhl] · *adjective*

When something is described as estival, it's related to summertime.

EUPHEMISM

[yoo-fuh-miz-uhm] · *noun*

A euphemism is a nice or polite way of saying something, especially something that people don't like to talk about because it makes them feel uncomfortable or embarrassed.

EUPHORIA

[yoo-fohr-ee-uh] · *noun*

Euphoria is a very intense feeling of happiness.

EXACERBATE

[ig-zas-er-beyt] · *verb*

When something exacerbates a bad situation, it makes it much worse than it already was.

EXTEMPORANEOUS

[ik-stem-puh-rey-nee-uhs] · *adjective*

When someone makes an extemporaneous speech, they do it off-the-cuff or without preparation.

ESTIVAL

Estival comes from the Latin word meaning *heat*.
If you describe a day in the spring as estival, this means
that it's warm and sunny, like it is in the summer. A related
word is *estivation*, which is kind of like hibernation, but it
happens during the summer and not the winter.

ICE CREAM

FACETIOUS

[fuh-**see**-shuhs] · *adjective*

If someone is being facetious, they are trying to be funny and make jokes in a situation where they should be acting seriously.

FANDANGO

[fan-**dang**-goh] · *noun*

The fandango is an energetic Spanish dance.

FESTINATE

[fes-tuh-neyt] · *verb*

When you festinate, you hurry or move very quickly.

FLAPDOODLE

[flap-dood-l] · *noun*

Flapdoodle is nonsense, or words and ideas that are absurd or ridiculous.

FLIBBERTIGIBBET

[flib-er-tee-jib-it] · *noun*

A flibbertigibbet is someone who is silly and likes to gossip or daydream.

FLOCCULENT

[**flok**-yuh-luhnt] · *adjective*

If something is flocculent, it is soft and fluffy like a clump of wool.

FLOTSAM

[flot-suhm] · *noun*

Flotsam are the pieces of a ship that float in the sea and wash up to the shore after a shipwreck.

FLUMMOX

[fluhm-uhks] · *verb*

When something flummoxes you, it makes you feel confused.

FORTUITOUS

[fahr-**too**-i-tuhs] · *adjective*

Something that is fortuitous is a good and lucky thing that happens unexpectedly.

FOURSCORE

[fohr-skohr] · *noun*

Fourscore is an old-fashioned way to say the number 80. When people use this word, they are usually quoting something that was written a long time ago.

FRABJOUS

[frab-juhs] · *adjective*

Something that is frabjous is wonderful, joyous, and amazing. This word was made up by Lewis Carroll, the author of *Alice in Wonderland*.

FRAZZLED

[**fraz**-uhld] · *adjective*

When someone is frazzled, they feel tired, overwhelmed, or exhausted.

FRENETIC

[fruh-**net**-ik] · *adjective*

When something is frenetic, it's energetic and fast, and usually not very controlled.

FUNAMBULIST

[fuh-**nam**-byuh-list] · *noun*

A funambulist is a tightrope walker.

FUNICULAR

[fuh-**nik**-yuh-ler] · *noun*

A funicular is a type of train that goes up the side of a very steep hill or a mountain.

FUNAMBULIST

There are records of funambulists from ancient times. Famous ancient Roman authors wrote about the funambulist performances they attended. Illustrations from this period show funambulists gracefully walking across tightropes while doing difficult tasks, like playing musical instruments.

GABFEST

[**gab**-fest] · *noun*

A gabfest is a casual conversation that's usually about fun or entertaining things. Sometimes people use this word when they're talking about gossip.

GAGGLE

[**gag**-uhl] · *noun*

A gaggle is a flock of geese.

GALE

[geyl] · *noun*

A gale is a very strong wind.

GARGANTUAN

[gahr-**gan**-choo-*uhn*] · *adjective*

If something is gargantuan, it is enormous.

GARGOYLE

[gahr-goil] · *noun*

A gargoyle is a stone statue that looks like a frightening or ugly creature. Gargoyles appear on older buildings and are often part of the water-draining system.

GELATINOUS

[juh-**lat**-n-uhs] · *adjective*

If something is gelatinous, it is thick, sticky, and wet, like jam.

GENEALOGY

[jee-nee-**al**-uh-jee] · *noun*

Genealogy is the study of family histories. In genealogy, family trees show different generations of a family and how everyone is related to one another.

GESTICULATE

[je-**stik**-yuh-leyt] · *verb*

If you gesticulate when you're talking, you use hand and arm movements or gestures to express yourself. You can gesticulate without saying anything out loud.

GLOCKENSPIEL

[**glok**-*uhn*-shpeel] · *noun*

A glockenspiel is a type of musical instrument. It's similar to a xylophone, but the keys are made out of metal.

GONDOLA

[**gon**-**duh**-*luh*] · *noun*

A gondola is a long, narrow boat used in long, narrow bodies of water, like canals. It's moved by someone who stands at one end with a pole or an oar.

GONZO

[**gon**-zoh] · *adjective*

If a story in the news is written in a gonzo style, the reporter talks more about their feelings or reactions to something than about facts or what actually happened.

GOURMAND

[**goor**-mahnd] · *noun*

A gourmand is someone who really enjoys food, and sometimes eats too much.

GRANDILOQUENT

[gran-**dil**-*uh*-kwuhnt] · *adjective*

If someone speaks in a grandiloquent style, they use big words and say things in a fancy way, usually because they're showing off.

GRIMOIRE

[greem-**wahr**] · *noun*

A grimoire is a book of magic spells that witches and wizards use.

Magic

GROTTO

[**grot**-oh] · *noun*

A grotto is a small cave, sometimes one that is built by people as decoration in a garden.

GONDOLA

In addition to being a type of boat, a gondola is also a form of transportation that moves through the air, high above the ground. It has a cabin that hangs from a thick cord, or a cable. People go up and down mountains in it.

HABERDASHERY

[**hab**-er-dash-*uh*-ree] · *noun*

When someone uses the word haberdashery, they are talking about small things used to make clothing, like buttons, thread, and zippers.

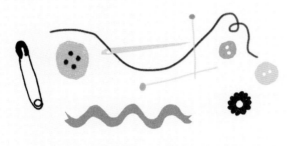

HAGIOGRAPHY

[hag-ee-**og**-ruh-fee] · *noun*

A hagiography is a book about someone that only says very positive things about them. The first hagiographies were stories about the lives of saints.

HA-HA

[hah-hah] · *noun*

A ha-ha is a type of fence that is dug into the ground around a garden or park, so it's hard to see. This is so the garden or park looks larger than it is.

HAPPENSTANCE

[**hap**-uhn-stans] · *noun*

If something occurs by happenstance, it's a coincidence and there's no real reason why it happened.

HARBINGER

[**hahr**-bin-jer] · *noun*

A harbinger of something is a sign that it will happen soon. Dark clouds can be a harbinger of a storm and flowers can be a harbinger of spring.

HEYDAY

[**hey**-dey] · *noun*

Someone's heyday is the time when they were most successful and popular. Things can also have heydays.

HIPPOPHILE

[**hip**-uh-fahyl] · *noun*

A hippophile is someone who loves horses.

HIRSUTE

[hur-**soot**] · *adjective*

Someone who is hirsute has lots of hair all over their body.

HISTRIONIC

[his-tree-**on**-ik] · *adjective*

If someone is being histrionic, they are being dramatic and emotional in a way that seems exaggerated and fake.

HOBNOB

[**hob**-nob] · *verb*

If you hobnob with others, especially rich and powerful people, you are friendly with them.

HOMAGE

[**hom**-ij] · *noun*

Homage is respect that someone shows to people or things that inspire them.

HOROLOGIST

[hoh-**rol**-uh-jist] · *noun*

A horologist is someone who makes and fixes clocks.

HUMDINGER

[**huhm**-ding-er] · *noun*

A humdinger is an exciting and amazing person or thing.

HUMDRUM

[**huhm**-druhm] · *adjective*

If something is humdrum, it's extremely boring.

HURDY-GURDY

[**hur**-dee-**gur**-dee] · *noun*

A hurdy-gurdy is a type of musical instrument with strings, a keyboard, and a crank.

HYPERBOLE

[hahy-**pur**-buh-lee] · *noun*

If someone uses hyperbole, they are exaggerating or saying something is much bigger, smaller, better, or worse than it really is. To say that a very tall person is 1,000 feet tall is an example of hyperbole.

HURDY-GURDY

A hurdy-gurdy is a stringed instrument like a violin, but you don't play it with a bow. You play a hurdy-gurdy by turning a crank while pressing keys. Not many people play the hurdy-gurdy today, though it was very popular in the past.

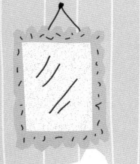

IANTHINE

[ahy-**an**-thin] · *adjective*

Something that is ianthine is the color violet.

ICEBLINK

[**ahys**-blingk] · *noun*

An iceblink is a patch of brightness in the sky over the sea. It's caused by the reflection of light from a large piece of ice.

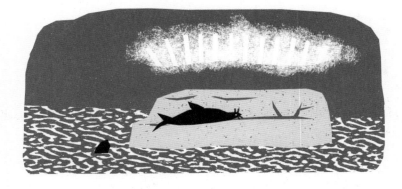

ICHTHYOLOGIST

[ik-thee-**ol**-*uh*-jist] · *noun*

An ichthyologist is someone who studies fish.

IDIOLECT

[**id**-ee-*uh*-lekt] · *noun*

An idiolect is the way that someone speaks that is unique to them and them alone.

IKEBANA

[ik-*uh*-**bah**-nuh] · *noun*

Ikebana is the Japanese art of arranging flowers in a beautiful way.

IMAGINEER

[ih-maj-*uh*-**neer**] · *noun*

An imagineer is someone who turns creative ideas into reality.

IMMINENT

[**im**-*uh*-nuhnt] · *adjective*

When something is imminent, it's expected to happen very soon.

IMMORTALIZE

[ih-**mohr**-tl-ahyz] · *verb*

When someone is immortalized in a song, painting, or other work of art, they are in it, and they will be remembered for a very long time because of it.

INANE

[ih-**neyn**] · *adjective*

If a question, idea, or behavior is inane, it's silly and foolish.

INDEFATIGABLE

[in-di-**fat**-i-*guh*-buhl] · *adjective*

Someone who is indefatigable never gets tired and always has the energy to do things.

INEFFABLE

[in-**ef**-*uh*-buhl] · *adjective*

When something is ineffable, it is too wonderful to be described by words.

INSIPID

[in-**sip**-id] · *adjective*

If someone has an insipid personality, they are boring. Food that is insipid doesn't have much flavor.

INTERROBANG

[in-**ter**-*uh*-bang] · *noun*

An interrobang is a punctuation mark that combines the exclamation mark with the question mark. It's used when someone is surprised or really excited while asking a question.

IRREVERENT

[ih-**rev**-er-*uhnt*] · *adjective*

When someone is irreverent, they might make fun of things that are usually taken very seriously.

IZZARD

[**iz**-erd] · *noun*

Izzard is an old-fashioned way to say the letter Z.

INDEFATIGABLE

People can be indefatigable, and so can things. For example, if someone runs a race, studies, and then makes dinner, they might be called indefatigable. If a ship moves quickly and never breaks down or sinks, it might be called indefatigable.

BOOK

poems

1000

JABBER

[jab-er] · *verb*

If you jabber, you talk quickly and make no sense.

JACKANAPES

[jak-*uh*-neyps] · *noun*

A jackanapes is someone who is impolite and disrespectful. A jackanapes can also be a child who has a lot of energy and likes to cause trouble.

JAMBOREE

[jam-*buh*-**ree**] · *noun*

A jamboree is a party, usually one that is big and loud.

JARGON

[jahr-*guhn*] · *noun*

When someone uses the word jargon, they're talking about the special words and expressions used by a specific group, usually a group of people who do the same job. People outside this group don't understand these words.

JEJUNE

[ji-**joon**] · *adjective*

Someone or something that is jejune is boring and not very important.

JEOPARDY

[**jep**-er-dee] · *noun*

If something is in jeopardy, it is in danger of not working out as planned.

JEST

[jest] · *noun*

If you say something in jest, you're saying it as a joke.

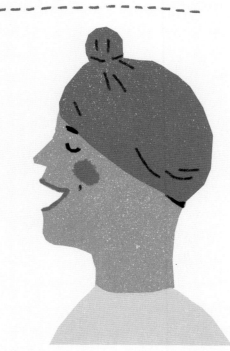

JILLION

[jil-*yuhn*] · *noun*

When someone uses the word jillion, they want to talk about a very large number, but they don't want to say an exact number.

JILT

[jilt] · *verb*

If you jilt someone, you end a romantic relationship with

them quickly and in an upsetting way.

JOBBERNOWL

[**job**-er-nohl] · *noun*

A jobbernowl is someone who is foolish and not very smart.

JOSTLE

[**jos**-*uhl*] · *verb*

If someone jostles you in a crowd, they bump up

against you or push you to get past.

JUBILANT

[**joo**-buh-luhnt] · *adjective*

When someone is jubilant, they are extremely happy because of a triumph or success. Someone might feel jubilant after winning a game.

JUGGERNAUT

[**juhg**-er-not] · *noun*

A juggernaut is a large and powerful object or force that destroys things.

JUVENILIA

[joo-vuh-**nil**-yuh] · *noun*

The juvenilia of a writer or artist is the work that they create before they've fully developed the style they're known for. This work is created when they're a child, teenager, or young adult.

JUXTAPOSE

[**juhk**-stuh-pohz] · *verb*

When you juxtapose two things, you place them next to each other so it's easy to see all the ways that they're different.

JUXTAPOSE

An artist might juxtapose dark and light colors, and a musician might juxtapose slow and fast parts of a song. A writer might juxtapose ideas like happiness and sadness.

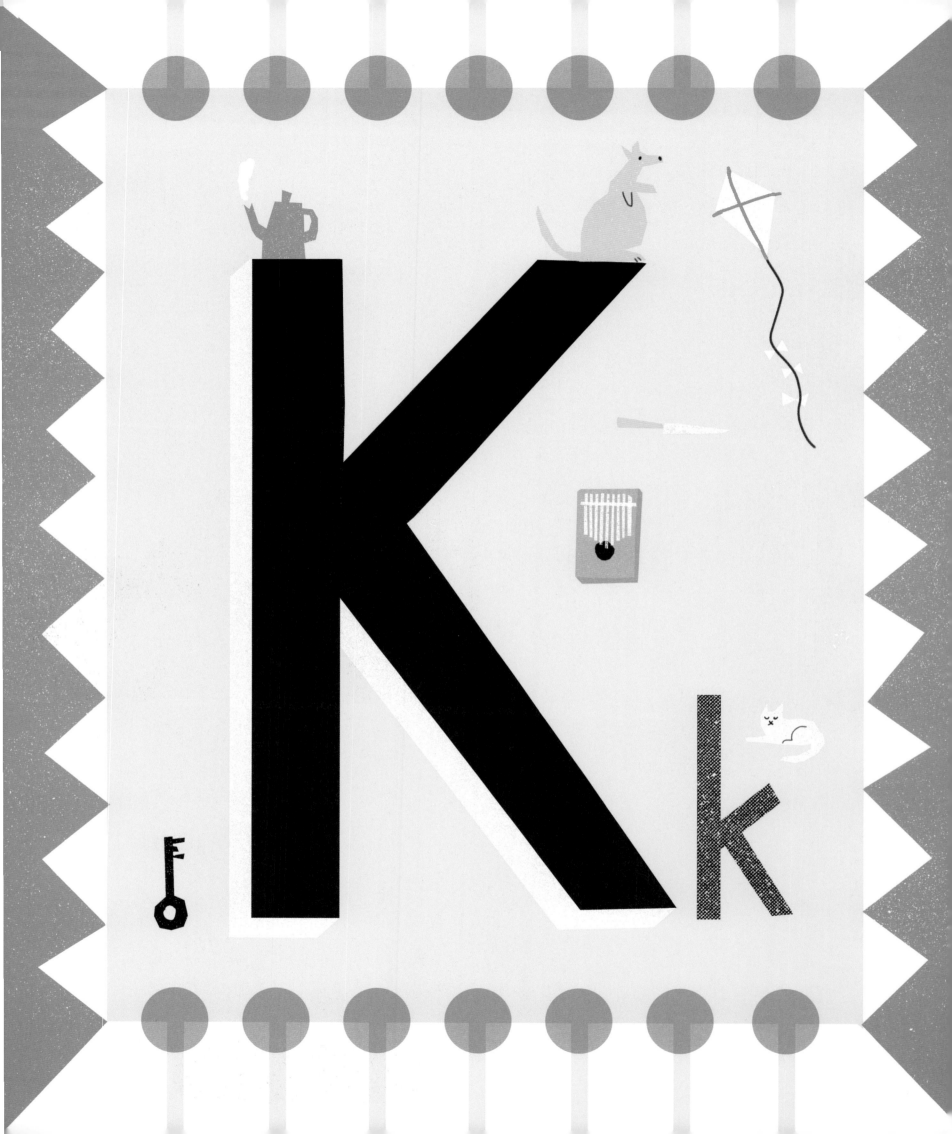

KAKISTOCRACY

[kak-*uh*-**stok**-ruh-see] · *noun*

Kakistocracy is government ruled by the worst people.

KALEIDOSCOPE

[kuh-**lahy**-*duh*-skohp] · *noun*

A kaleidoscope is a tube that has small, colorful chips and mirrors at one end. When someone looks into the other end, they see beautiful patterns that change as they turn the tube.

KALIMBA

[kuh-**lim**-*buh*] · *noun*

A kalimba is a small musical instrument with metal keys. It's played with the thumbs and is sometimes called a thumb piano.

KAPUT

[kah-**poot**] · *adjective*

If something goes kaput, it doesn't work anymore.

KARAOKE

[kar-ee-**oh**-kee] · *noun*

Karaoke is when people sing songs into a microphone for fun, while a machine plays the music.

KENSPECKLE

[**ken**-spek-*uhl*] · *adjective*

If something is kenspeckle, it's easy to recognize or easy to see.

KERFUFFLE

[ker-**fuhf**-*uhl*] · *noun*

A kerfuffle is a noisy and confusing thing that happens.

KINETIC

[ki-**net**-ik] · *adjective*

When someone uses the word kinetic, they are talking about what makes things start and stop moving.

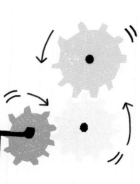

KISMET

[**kiz**-met] · *noun*

When someone talks about kismet, they're talking about fate, or what they believe controls everything that happens in the universe.

KNACK

[nak] · *noun*

A knack is a special skill or talent that someone has.

KNAPSACK

[**nap**-sak] · *noun*

A knapsack is a backpack.

KNAVE

[neyv] · *noun*

A knave is someone who is dishonest and cannot be trusted.

KNEE-SLAPPER

[**nee**-slap-er] · *noun*

A knee-slapper is a joke or story that is extremely funny and makes others laugh very hard.

ha ha ha!

KRAKEN

[krah-*kuhn*] · *noun*

The kraken is a legendary Norwegian sea monster.

KVETCH

[kvech] · *verb*

When you kvetch about something, you complain about it.

KRAKEN

According to legend, the kraken is so large that it can be mistaken for an island. While there have been many reported sightings over the years, there is no proof of the kraken's existence. Scientists believe that when people thought they were seeing the kraken, they were actually looking at a giant squid, which can grow to be up to 43 feet long.

LABORIOUS

[luh-**bohr**-ee-uhs] · *adjective*

Something that is laborious is very difficult and takes a lot of time and careful attention.

LABYRINTH

[**lab**-uh-rinth] · *noun*

A labyrinth is a maze, or something that is very easy to get lost in.

LACKADAISICAL

[lak-uh-**dey**-zi-kuhl] · *adjective*

If someone is lackadaisical, they do not seem excited or interested in the things they do.

LEAFDOM

[**leef**-duhm] · *noun*

A leafdom is an area with a lot of plants and leaves that feels like its own world.

LEXICOGRAPHER

[lek-si-**kog**-ruh-fer] · *noun*

A lexicographer is someone who writes and edits dictionaries.

LINCHPIN

[**linch**-pin] · *noun*

The linchpin of something is the person or thing that holds it all together, or the most important part of something.

LIONIZE

[**lahy**-uh-nahyz] · *verb*

When you lionize someone, you treat them as if they are very important and special.

LOLLAPALOOZA

[lol-*uh*-p*uh*-**loo**-zuh] · *noun*

A lollapalooza is a person, thing, or event that is extraordinary or impressive.

LOLLYGAG

[**lol**-ee-gag] · *verb*

If you lollygag around, you are not doing anything when there's probably something you should be doing.

LOVELORN

[**luhv**-lohrn] · *adjective*

When someone is lovelorn, they're sad because they're in love with someone who doesn't love them back.

LUDDITE

[**luhd**-ahyt] · *noun*

A luddite is someone who is against using new technologies.

LUGUBRIOUS

[loo-**goo**-bree-uhs] · *adjective*

Someone or something that is lugubrious is extremely sad and mournful.

LUMINOUS

[loo-muh-nuhs] · *adjective*

When something is luminous, it's bright, shining, and full of light.

LUTE

[loot] · *noun*

A lute is a musical instrument with strings and a pear-shaped body.

LYCANTHROPE

[**lahy**-kuhn-throhp] · *noun*

A lycanthrope is a werewolf.

LEXICOGRAPHER

LexiCographers study how people use words, and then they write down what they learn in diCtionaries. Though it doesn't always feel like it, language is Constantly Changing and growing. Sometimes people invent new words, and sometimes old words get new meanings.

jane

MASTICATE

[mas-ti-keyt] · *verb*

When you masticate food, you chew it.

MAUDLIN

[mawd-lin] · *adjective*

Someone or something that is maudlin is too sentimental or emotional.

MAVEN

[mey-vuhn] · *noun*

A maven is someone who knows a lot about a subject or is extremely good at something.

MAVERICK

[mav-rik] · *noun*

A maverick is someone who is independent and has their own way of doing things.

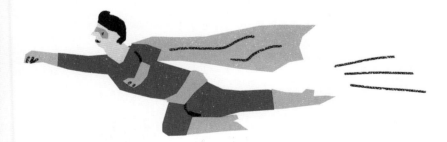

MAXIM

[mak-sim] · *noun*

A maxim is a short saying that gives advice on how to live your life. For example, *Don't put all your eggs in one basket* means that you should always have a back-up plan in case something doesn't work out.

METAGROBOLIZE

[met-uh-grob-uh-lahyz] · *verb*

If you are metagrobolized by something, you are puzzled or confused by it. People use this word when they want to be funny.

MICROCOSM

[mahy-kruh-koz-uhm] · *noun*

A microcosm is a small thing that can represent something that is much bigger.

MINOTAUR

[min-*uh*-tawr] · *noun*

The Minotaur is a mythological monster with the head of a bull and the body of a man.

MIRTH

[murth] · *noun*

If someone is filled with mirth, they think something is so entertaining that they laugh with joy.

MISCELLANEOUS

[mis-*uh*-**ley**-nee-*uhs*] · *adjective*

Something that's miscellaneous is hard to put into one category or another.

MISHPOCHA

[mish-**pookh**-uh] · *noun*

Someone's mishpocha is their family and very close friends.

MOONBOW

[moon-boh] · *noun*

A moonbow is a nighttime rainbow that's made from the light of the Moon.

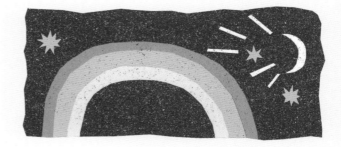

MUGWUMP

[**muhg**-wuhmp] · *noun*

A mugwump is someone who has a hard time making decisions. People often use this word when they're talking about politicians.

MULLIGRUBS

[**muhl**-i-gruhbz] · *noun*

If someone has the mulligrubs, they feel very sad and are in a bad mood.

MUMPSIMUS

[muhmp-*suh*-muhs] · *noun*

A mumpsimus is a person who believes something because they've always believed it, even though it's wrong or makes no sense.

MINOTAUR

According to Greek mythology, the Minotaur lived in the center of a giant labyrinth, or maze. Some stories say he had the head of a bull and the body of a man, but some say it was the other way around. He was killed by Theseus, who later became King of Athens.

NADIR

[**ney**-der] . *noun*

The nadir of something is the lowest or worst possible place it could be.

NAÏVE

[**nah**-eev] . *adjective*

If someone is naïve, they don't have a lot of life experience. They believe what they are told, even if it's not true, and they tend to trust people who are not very trustworthy.

NARWHAL

[**nahr**-wuhl] . *noun*

A narwhal is a type of whale that lives in the Arctic. Male narwhals have a long, twisted, and pointy tusk coming out of their heads.

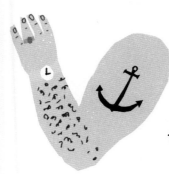

NAUTICAL

[**not**-i-kuhl] . *adjective*

If something is nautical, it's related to sailors, ships, or the sea.

NAYSAYER

[**ney**-sey-er] . *noun*

A naysayer is someone who says *no* a lot, and who often views things in a negative way.

NEBULOUS

[**neb**-yuh-luhs] . *adjective*

If an idea is nebulous, it's hard to describe because it's not completely clear what the idea is.

NEOLOGISM

[nee-**ol**-uh-jiz-uhm] . *noun*

A neologism is a new word or phrase.

NEPOTISM

[**nep**-uh-tiz-uhm] . *noun*

Nepotism is when powerful people give jobs to their family and close friends, whether or not those people deserve those jobs.

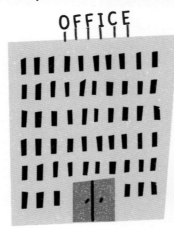

NEWFANGLED

[**noo**-fang-guhld] · *adjective*

When a person calls something newfangled, they're saying it's new in a way that they don't like because it's different from what they're used to.

NICTATE

[**nik**-teyt] · *verb*

When you nictate, you blink or wink.

NINNYHAMMER

[**nin**-ee-ham-er] · *noun*

A ninnyhammer is someone who is silly or foolish.

NOCTURNAL

[nok-**tur**-nl] · *adjective*

If something is nocturnal, it's related to the night.

NOISOME

[**noi**-suhm] · *adjective*

If something is noisome, it's very unpleasant or disgusting, like the smell of something rotting.

NOMADIC

[noh-**mad**-ik] · *adjective*

If a group is nomadic, they roam from place to place without a permanent home.

NONCHALANT

[non-shuh-**lahnt**] · *adjective*

When someone acts in a nonchalant way, they seem like they're calm and not worried.

NUCIVOROUS

[noo-**siv**-er-uhs] · *adjective*

If an animal is nucivorous, it eats nuts. Squirrels are nucivorous.

NOCTURNAL

Nocturnal animals are awake at night and sleep during the day. Bats are nocturnal, and they're the only mammals that can fly. To figure out where they're going, bats make high-pitched noises and listen to those sounds bounce off objects and walls. This is called *echolocation*.

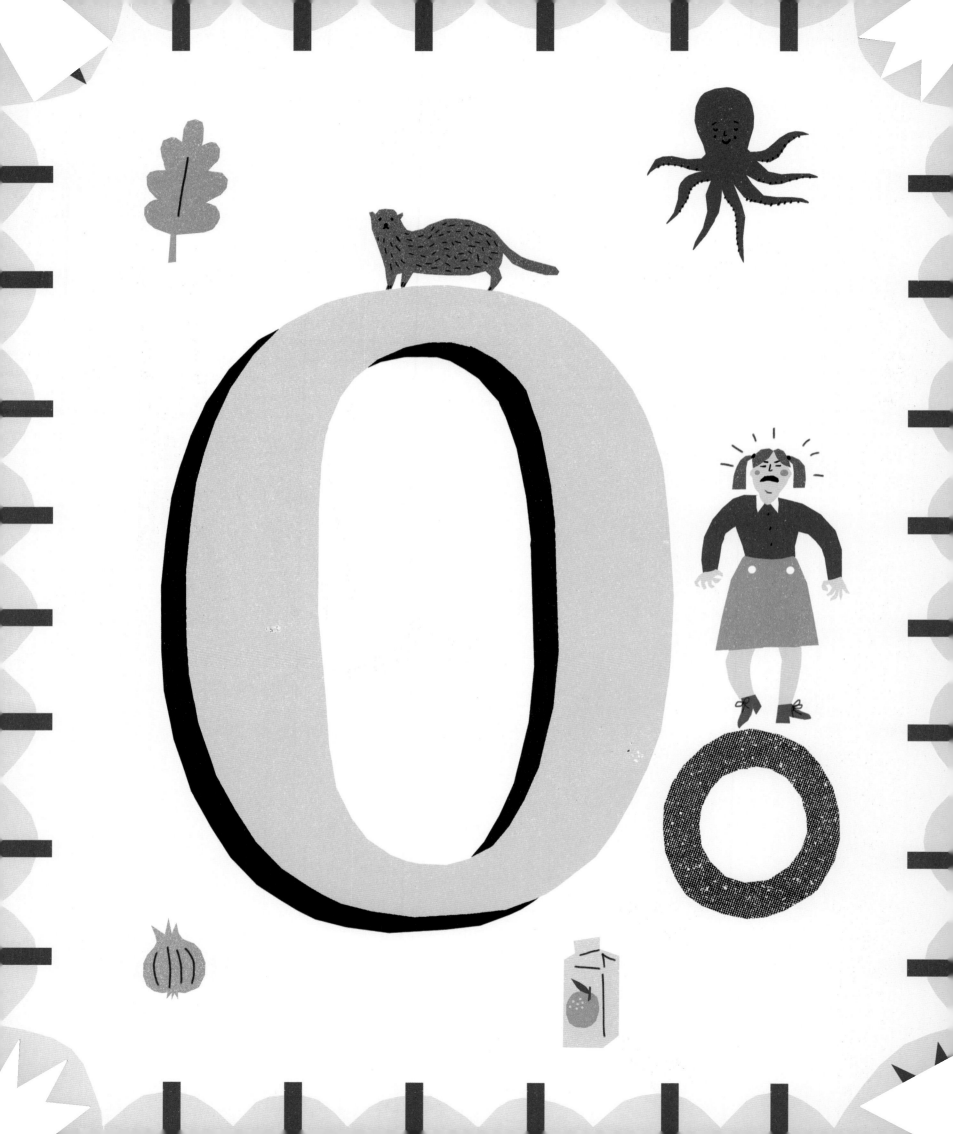

OBELISK

[**ob**-*uh*-lisk] · *noun*

An obelisk is a tall stone statue with a pointy top. They're often built in honor of an important person or event.

OBFUSCATE

[**ob**-*fuh*-skeyt] · *verb*

If you obfuscate something, you make it very confusing and hard to understand on purpose.

OBSOLETE

[ob-*suh*-**leet**] · *adjective*

If something is obsolete, it is not used anymore because something newer or better has come along.

OGRE

[**oh**-ger] · *noun*

In fairy tales, an ogre is a giant monster.

OLFACTORY

[ol-**fak**-*tuh*-ree] · *adjective*

When someone uses the word olfactory, they're talking about the sense of smell.

OMBUDSMAN

[**om**-*buhdz*-*muhn*] · *noun*

The job of an ombudsman is to research complaints people have about an organization or government.

OMINOUS

[**om**-*uh*-nuhs] · *adjective*

If something is ominous, it makes people worry that something bad will happen.

OMNISCIENT

[om-**nish**-*uhnt*] · *adjective*

If someone is omniscient, they know everything. If a book has an omniscient narrator, the story is told from the point of view of different characters.

OMPHALOSCOPY

[**om**-*fuh*-*luh*-skohp-*ee*] · *noun*

Omphaloscopy is when someone focuses too much on one idea and never gets anything done, also known as *navel-gazing*. People use this word when they want to be funny.

ONEROUS

[**oh**-ner-uhs] · *adjective*
If someone thinks a task or responsibility is onerous, it is really hard to do, and they don't like doing it.

ONOMATOPOEIA

[on-*uh*-mah-*tuh*-**pee**-*uh*] · *noun*

An onomatopoeia is a word that sounds like a noise when you say it aloud.

OOLOGY

[oh-**ol**-*uh*-jee] · *noun*
Oology is the study of eggs, especially birds' eggs.

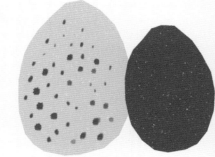

OPAQUE

[oh-**peyk**] · *adjective*

If something is opaque, you can't see through it. If an idea is opaque, it's hard to understand.

ORNERY

[**ohr**-nuh-ree] · *adjective*
If someone is ornery, they are difficult to be around and they're always in a bad mood.

ORTHOGRAPHY

[ohr-**thog**-ruh-fee] · *noun*

When someone uses the word orthography, they're talking about how to spell words correctly.

ONOMATOPOEIA

Cows *moo*, horses *neigh*, birds *tweet*, frogs *ribbit*, mice *squeak*, and sheep *baa*. In different languages, animals make different sounds. In English the onomatopoeia for the sound a cat makes is *meow*, and in Japanese it's *nyan*.

PALINDROME

[**pal**-in-drohm] · *noun*

A palindrome is a word or phrase that, when read backward, spells the same word or phrase. *Pop, noon, racecar,* and *Was it a bat I saw?* are all palindromes.

Was it a bat I saw?

PARADIGM

[**par**-*uh*-dahym] · *noun*

A paradigm is the typical example or model of what a thing is. If something is called a paradigm shift, it is a

EUREKA!

new way of thinking that changes how people view the world.

PENULTIMATE

[pi-**nuhl**-*tuh*-mit] · *adjective*

When someone uses the word penultimate, they're talking about the second to last thing in a list or series.

PERENNIAL

[puh-**ren**-ee-uhl] · *adjective*

If something is perennial, it happens every year or it is always happening. Perennial flowers bloom from the same plant year after year.

PETRICHOR

[pe-**trahy**-kohr] · *noun*

Petrichor is the earthy smell that comes from rain falling on soil, especially after it hasn't rained in a while.

PHANTASMAGORIC

[fan-taz-*muh*-**gor**-ik] · *adjective*

If something is phantasmagoric, it's like a fantasy from a dream.

PIEBALD

[**pahy**-bawld] · *adjective*

If an animal is piebald, it has patches of black and white fur.

PITHY

[**pith**-ee] · *adjective*

When you say something that's pithy, it's short, to the point, and full of meaning.

PLETHORA

[**pleth**-er-*uh*] · *noun*

A plethora of something is a large amount of that thing—usually more than is wanted or needed.

POLYMATH

[**pol**-ee-math] · *noun*

A polymath is someone who is very good at learning and knows a lot about different subjects.

PORTMANTEAU

[pohrt-man-**toh**] · *noun*

A portmanteau is when two or more words squeeze into one new word.

PRECOCIOUS

[pri-**koh**-shuhs] · *adjective*

If a child is precocious, they are a very fast learner who knows things that kids their age don't usually know.

PRESTIDIGITATION

[pres-ti-dij-i-**tey**-shuhn] · *noun*

Prestidigitation is the art of moving your hands skillfully, so others think they're seeing something that they're not actually seeing.

PUGNACIOUS

[puhg-**ney**-shuhs] · *adjective*

Someone who is pugnacious is always arguing or fighting with others.

PULCHRITUDINOUS

[puhl-kri-**tood**-n-*uh*s] · *adjective*

If someone is pulchritudinous, they are very beautiful.

PORTMANTEAU

Brunch is a portmanteau that combines the words *breakfast* and *lunch*, and *spork* combines the words *spoon* and *fork*. Some dog breed names are portmanteaus. A puggle is part pug and part beagle. A labradoodle is part labrador retriever and part poodle.

GASTROPU

CRONUTS

QIVIUT

[**kee**-vee-*uht*] · *noun*

Qiviut is the soft fuzzy hair on a musk ox that is under its longer layer of hair. Musk oxen live in the Arctic, a very cold environment, and they shed their qiviut in the warmer months.

QUACKSALVER

[**kwak**-sal-ver] · *noun*

A quacksalver is someone who says that they have skills or knowledge that they don't actually have.

QUAGMIRE

[**kwag**-mahy*uhr*] · *noun*

A quagmire is a confusing and complicated situation that's hard to get out of. A quagmire is also an area of land that's so soft and squishy that you sink into it when you walk there.

QUAINT

[**kweynt**] · *adjective*

When something is quaint, it's charming or cute in an old-fashioned way.

QUANDARY

[**kwon**-dree] · *noun*

If someone is in a quandary, they have to make a decision but they're not sure what the right decision is.

QUARANTINE

[**kwor**-*uhn*-teen] · *noun*

If someone who is sick is put in quarantine, they are separated from others for a period of time to stop the spread of disease.

QUARRELSOME

[**kwor**-*uhl*-suhm] · *adjective*

If someone is quarrelsome, they often get into fights with others.

QUIBBLE

[**kwib**-*uhl*] · *verb*

When people quibble, they're having a pointless argument about something that doesn't really matter. A quibble is also a complaint about something that is not important at all.

QUIDNUNC

[**kwid**-nuhngk] · *noun*

A quidnunc is someone who is very nosy and likes to gossip about the lives of other people.

QUILL

[kwil] · *noun*

A quill is a type of pen that's made out of the feather of a bird.

QUINQUENNIUM

[kwin-**kwen**-ee-*uhm*] · *noun*

A quinquennium is a period of five years.

QUIP

[kwip] · *noun*

A quip is a clever thing that someone says.

QUIVER

[**kwiv**-er] · *verb*

If something quivers, it trembles or shakes a small amount at a fast speed.

QUIXOTIC

[kwik-**sot**-ik] · *adjective*

If an idea is quixotic, it's wonderful, but it's not very realistic.

QUOTIDIAN

[kwoh-**tid**-ee-*uhm*] · *adjective*

If an activity is quotidian, it's a regular everyday thing that happens all the time.

QUAINT

Quaint is often used to describe small towns or villages and the houses and shops in them. However, this is not what quaint originally meant when people first started using it, about 800 years ago. Back then it was used to describe a clever person who was very good at tricking others.

RAMBUNCTIOUS

[ram-**buhngk**-shuhs] · *adjective*

If someone is rambunctious, they have a lot of energy and are being very noisy because they're excited and happy.

sqwawk!

RAMFEEZLED

[ram-**fee**-zuhld] · *adjective*

If someone is ramfeezled, they are worn out and exhausted.

RAPSCALLION

[rap-**skal**-yuhn] · *noun*

A rapscallion is someone who is dishonest and is always causing trouble.

RAVENOUS

[**rav**-uh-nuhs] · *adjective*

If someone is ravenous, they are very hungry.

REBUS

[**ree**-buhs] · *noun*

A rebus is a puzzle that uses pictures, symbols, and letters to represent sounds and words. For example, an image of a bee next to an image of a leaf might be used to mean the word *believe*.

REDOLENT

[**red**-l-uhnt] · *adjective*

If something is redolent of something else, it reminds you of that thing.

REPLICA

[**rep**-li-kuh] · *noun*

A replica is a copy of something—often a piece of art.

RESPLENDENT

[ri-**splen**-duhnt] · *adjective*

When something is resplendent, it sparkles and shines. If a person is resplendent, they look so beautiful, it's as if they're glowing.

RETICENT

[**ret**-uh-suhnt] · *adjective*

Someone who is reticent doesn't usually talk about what they're thinking or how they're feeling.

REVEL

[**rev**-uhl] · *verb*

If you revel in something, you feel happiness and joy when you experience it.

REVERIE

[**rev**-uh-ree] · *noun*

A reverie is a dreamlike thought that you have when you're awake.

RHETORICAL

[ri-**tor**-i-kuhl] · *adjective*

A rhetorical question is a question that is not meant to be answered, often because there is no right answer.

RIFE

[rahyf] · *adjective*

If a place is rife with something, that thing is extremely common in that place. If a town is rife with cats, there are cats everywhere you look.

RIPSNORTER

[rip-**snohr**-ter] · *noun*

A ripsnorter is something that's extraordinary and amazing.

ROSARIUM

[roh-**zair**-ee-uhm] · *noun*

A rosarium is a rose garden.

ROTUND

[roh-**tuhnd**] · *adjective*

Something that is rotund is round or rounded.

REPLICA

An artist might create a replica of a painting they love in order to understand how that work was made. This can help them learn new techniques for their own paintings.

SUCCESSFUL FORGERY

How to paint like Leo.

SALUBRIOUS

[suh-**loo**-bree-uhs] · *adjective*

If something is salubrious, it's enjoyable and good for your health.

SCARAMOUCH

[**skar**-*uh*-mouch] · *noun*

A scaramouch is a cowardly and dishonest person.

SCHADENFREUDE

[**shahd**-n-froi-duh] · *noun*

Schadenfreude is when someone feels extremely happy when bad things happen to other people.

SERENDIPITY

[ser-*uhn*-**dip**-i-tee] · *noun*

Serendipity is the luck someone has when they discover something fun or interesting without looking for it.

SESQUIPEDALIAN

[ses-kwi-pi-**dey**-lee-*uhn*] · *adjective*

If someone is sesquipedalian, they know a lot of big words and they love using them.

SIDEREAL

[sahy-**deer**-ee-uhl] · *adjective*

When something is sidereal, it's related to the stars.

SKULDUGGERY

[skuhl-**duhg**-*uh*-ree] · *noun*

Skulduggery is dishonest behavior that's used to trick and take advantage of others.

SLUGABED

[**sluhg**-*uh*-bed] · *noun*

A slugabed is someone who is lazy and loves sleeping in late when they should be awake.

SMORGASBORD

[**shmohr**-*guhs*-bawrd] · *noun*

A smorgasbord is a wide variety of things that can all be found together in one place.

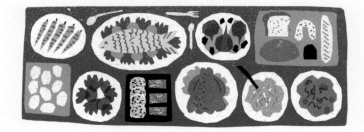

SNUGGERY

[**snuhg**-uh-ree] · *noun*

A snuggery is a comfortable and cozy place.

SOCKDOLAGER

[sok-**dol**-uh-jer] · *noun*

A sockdolager is a very clever reply that wins an argument.

SOMNAMBULIST

[som-**nam**-byuh-list] · *noun*

A somnambulist is someone who walks in their sleep.

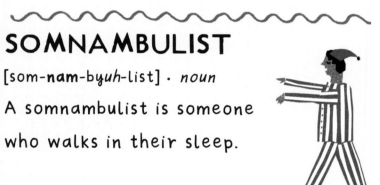

SPAGHETTIFICATION

[spuh-get-uh-fi-**key**-shuhn] · *noun*

Spaghettification is the idea that objects get long and skinny like spaghetti when they're sucked into black holes.

SPELUNKING

[spi-**luhngk**-ing] · *noun*

Spelunking is the hobby of exploring caves.

SPHINX

[sfingks] · *noun*

The sphinx is a mythological monster with the head of a human, the body of a lion, and wings. In stories, the sphinx asks people riddles.

SQUAMOUS

[**skwey**-muhs] · *adjective*

If something is squamous, it's covered with scales. Fish are squamous.

STERNUTATION

[stur-nyuh-**tey**-shuhn] · *noun*

Sternutation is when someone sneezes.

SPAGHETTIFICATION

Spaghettification could not exist without black holes. Black holes are spots in space that have a lot of gravity, and because of that, they pull anything nearby into them. Gravity is the same force that makes objects fall to the earth when we drop them.

TACITURN

[**tas**-i-turn] · *adjective*

Someone who is taciturn is very quiet and doesn't talk a lot.

TANDEM

[**tan**-duhm] · *adjective*

A tandem bicycle is a bicycle for two riders, where one rider sits behind the other.

TEMPESTUOUS

[tem-**pes**-choo-uhs] · *adjective*

A tempestuous relationship has a lot of strong emotions, fighting, and hurt feelings.

TESTUDINAL

[te-**stood**-n-l] · *adjective*

If something is testudinal, it's related to tortoises, turtles, or their shells.

THALASSIC

[thuh-**las**-ik] · *adjective*

Something that is thalassic is related to the sea.

THESPIAN

[**thes**-pee-uhn] · *noun*

A thespian is an actor.

THIGMOTROPISM

[thig-**mo**-truh-piz-uhm] · *noun*

Thigmotropism is the sense of touch that some plants have that makes them grow in spirals around things.

TINTINNABULUM

[tin-ti-**nab**-yuh-luhm] · *noun*

A tintinnabulum is a small bell.

TOME

[tohm] · *noun*

A tome is a very large and heavy book.

TRANSLUCENT

[trans-**loo**-suhnt] · *adjective*

If a window is translucent, you can see light through it, but you can't see exactly what's on the other side.

TRANSMOGRIFY

[trans-**mog**-ruh-fahy] · *verb*

If something has transmogrified, it's changed in a strange and surprising way.

TRISKAIDEKAPHOBIA

[tris-kuh-dek-uh-**foh**-bee-uh] · *noun*

Triskaidekaphobia is a fear of the number 13.

TROGLODYTE

[**trog**-luh-dahyt] · *noun*

A troglodyte is someone who lives in a cave.

TULIPOMANIA

[too-luh-puh-**mey**-nee-uh] · *noun*

When someone uses the word tulipomania, they're talking about Holland in the 1630s. At this time people were so excited about tulips that they became extremely expensive and people made and lost a lot of money buying and selling them.

TUROPHILE

[**t**oor-uh-fahyl] · *noun*

A turophile is a cheese lover, or someone who knows a lot about cheese.

TROGLODYTE

The first troglodytes were from prehistoric times. We know they lived in caves because they left paintings on their walls telling stories about their lives. A person might be called a troglodyte if they act as if they're from a different time and don't understand things other people understand.

UBIQUITOUS

[yoo-**bik**-wi-tuhs] · *adjective*

If something is ubiquitous, it's so common it feels like it's everywhere.

UFOLOGY

[yoo-**fol**-*uh*-jee] · *noun*

Ufology is the study of UFOs, or unidentified flying objects.

UGGLESOME

[**uhg**-*uhl*-suhm] · *adjective*

Something that is ugglesome is horrible and scary.

UKULELE

[yoo-kuh-**ley**-lee] · *noun*

A ukulele is a type of musical instrument. It's similar to a guitar, but it's smaller.

ULIGINOUS

[yoo-**lij**-*uh*-nuhs] · *adjective*

If a plant is uliginous, it grows in wet and swampy environments.

ULTRACREPIDARIAN

[uhl-truh-krep-i-**dair**-ee-uhn] · *noun*

An ultracrepidarian is someone who has big opinions about things they know nothing about.

UMBRAGE

[**uhm**-brij] · *noun*

If someone takes umbrage to something, they think it's rude or offensive.

UMBRIFEROUS

[uhm-**brif**-er-uhs] · *adjective*

If a tree is umbriferous, there is shade underneath it.

UMLAUT

[*oom*-lout] · *noun*

An umlaut is the two dots that appear over vowels in some languages.

UNCTUOUS

[**uhngk**-choo-uhs] · *adjective*

If someone is an unctuous person, they say extremely nice things, but they don't mean what they say.

UNDULATE

[**uhn**-juh-leyt] · *verb*

If something undulates, it moves back and forth like a wave.

UNKEMPT

[uhn-**kempt**] · *adjective*

When something is unkempt, it's very messy or dirty.

UPEND

[uhp-**end**] · *verb*

If something is upended, it's turned upside down.

URSINE

[**ur**-sahyn] · *adjective*

If something is ursine, it's related to, or like, a bear.

UTOPIA

[yoo-**toh**-pee-uh] · *noun*

A utopia is an imaginary place where everything is perfect.

UFOLOGY

Do aliens exist? And if they do, what sort of spacecraft would they use to travel around the universe? Ufologists believe aliens are out there, and they're especially interested in collecting evidence of their forms of transportation.

VAINGLORIOUS

[veyn-**glohr**-ee-uhs] · *adjective*

When someone is vainglorious, they have a very high opinion of themselves and they talk about how wonderful they are all the time.

VARIEGATED

[**vair**-ee-i-gey-tid] · *adjective*

If something is variegated, it has different patches or spots of color on it.

VERBOSE

[ver-**bohs**] · *adjective*

When someone is verbose, they use more words than needed to say something.

VERMILION

[ver-**mil**-yuhn] · *noun*

Vermilion is a bright red color.

VERNACULAR

[veh-**nak**-yuh-ler] · *noun*

The vernacular of a place is the language and style of speaking that people use in that place.

VERSATILE

[**vur**-suh-tl] · *adjective*

If something is versatile, it can be used in many different ways.

VIBRASLAP

[**vahy**-bruh-slap] · *noun*

A vibraslap is a musical instrument that makes a rattling noise when you hit it.

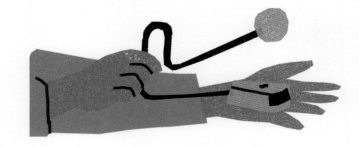

VILIFY

[**vil**-uh-fahy] · *verb*

If you vilify someone, you say bad things about them.

VISTA

[vis-*tuh*] · *noun*

A vista is the view from a beautiful place.

VOCIFEROUS

[voh-**sif**-er-*uh*s] · *adjective*

If someone is vociferous, they say their opinions in a loud and intense way.

VOID

[void] · *noun*

A void is a large and empty space.

VOLATILE

[vol-*uh*-tl] · *adjective*

If something is volatile, it's not predictable and it can change at any moment without warning.

VOLCANOLOGIST

[vol-*kuh*-**nol**-*uh*-jist] · *noun*

A volcanologist is someone who studies volcanoes.

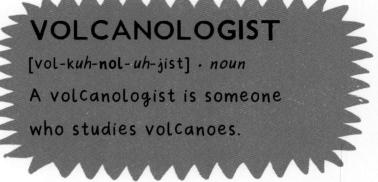

VOMITORIUM

[vom-i-**tohr**-ee-*uhm*] · *noun*

Vomitoriums are the passageways people used to enter and exit ancient Roman amphitheaters.

VOMITORIUM

VORTEX

[vohr-teks] · *noun*

A vortex is a spinning funnel of water or air that moves so fast that things are pulled into its center.

VOLCANOLOGIST

Volcanologists use their knowledge of geology to try and figure out when volcanoes might erupt. This is a very important job because it can help people who live near volcanoes understand when it's not safe for them to be in the area.

WANDERLUST

[**won**-der-luhst] · *noun*

Someone with wanderlust loves traveling. They often get bored if they stay in the same place for too long.

WHANGDOODLE

[**wang**-dood-l] · *noun*

A whangdoodle is an imaginary creature.

WHIMSICAL

[**wim**-zi-kuhl] · *adjective*

If something is whimsical, it's playful, fun, and imaginative.

WHIPPERSNAPPER

[**wip**-er-snap-er] · *noun*

A whippersnapper is someone who thinks they know a lot more than they actually do. Usually an older person uses this word about a younger person who they think has a lot to learn.

WHIZGIG

[**wiz**-gig] · *noun*

A whizgig is something that spins around very quickly, like a spinning top.

WILY

[**wahy**-lee] · *adjective*

If someone is wily, they are good at tricking others.

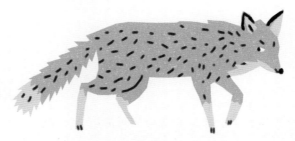

WINSOME

[**win**-suhm] · *adjective*

If someone is winsome, they are charming. A winsome smile is a warm and pleasant smile.

WISECRACK

[**wahyz**-krak] · *noun*

A wisecrack is a joke.

WISHY-WASHY

[**wish**-ee-waw-shee] · *adjective*

If someone is wishy-washy, they're not sure what they want, and they have trouble making decisions.

WORMHOLE

[**wurm**-hohl] · *noun*

A wormhole is a tunnel in space that connects one area of the universe to another.

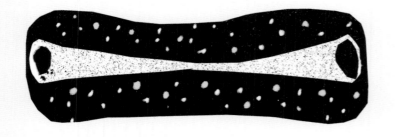

WORRYWART

[**wur**-ee-wohrt] · *noun*

A worrywart is someone who spends a lot of time thinking about all the ways things could go wrong.

WRACKFUL

[**rak**-fuhl] · *adjective*

If something is wrackful, it causes destruction.

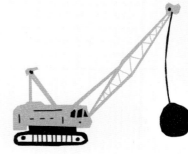

WRANGLE

[**rang**-guhl] · *verb*

When people wrangle with each other, they argue loudly.

WUNDERKIND

[**voon**-der-kind] · *noun*

A wunderkind is a child with amazing talents and abilities. A wunderkind is also a younger adult who is successful in whatever they do.

WUTHERING

[**wuhth**-er-ing] · *adjective*

If a place is wuthering, there are strong winds there.

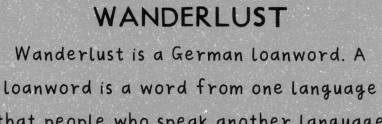

WANDERLUST

Wanderlust is a German loanword. A loanword is a word from one language that people who speak another language borrow and start using. This is sometimes because there's no good way of saying the same thing in the other language.

X

[eks] · *verb*

If you x something out, you cross it out.

XANADU

[**zan**-*uh*-doo] · *noun*

A Xanadu is a place that is so beautiful and perfect that it seems like it's from a dream.

XANTHIC

[**zan**-thik] · *adjective*

Something that is xanthic is the color yellow.

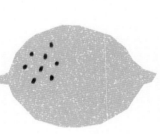

XEBEC

[**zee**-bek] · *noun*

A xebec is a type of sailing ship with three masts.

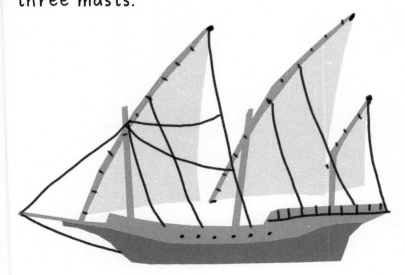

XENIAL

[**zee**-nee-*uhl*] · *adjective*

When something is xenial, it's about the relationship between a host and their guests.

XENIZATION

[zen-*uh*-**zey**-shuhn] · *noun*

When someone uses the word xenization, they're talking about a person's travels as a stranger.

XENOPHOBIA

[zee-nuh-**foh**-bee-*uh*] · *noun*

Xenophobia is the fear or hatred of people from other countries.

XERISCAPE

[**zeer**-i-skeyp] · *noun*

A xeriscape is a garden with plants that grow in very dry climates. People create xeriscapes to save water.

XERUS

[**zeer**-uhs] · *noun*

A xerus is a type of squirrel that lives in Africa.

XESTURGY

[**zes**-tur-jee] · *noun*

When someone uses the word xesturgy, they're talking about polishing objects, like stones.

XIPH

[zif] · *noun*

Xiph is an old name for the swordfish.

XIPHOID

[**zif**-oid] · *adjective*

If something is xiphoid, it's shaped like a sword.

X-RAY

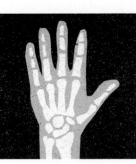

[**eks**-rey] · *noun*

An X-ray is a special type of picture that shows the inside of things. Doctors use X-rays to look at bones inside our bodies.

XYLOGRAPHY

[zahy-**log**-ruh-fee] · *noun*

Xylography is the art of carving a design or image into wood.

XYLOPHONE

[**zahy**-luh-fohn] · *noun*

A xylophone is a type of musical instrument. It's similar to a glockenspiel, but the keys are made out of wood.

XYST

[zist] · *noun*

A xyst is a long garden walkway with trees, which people used for exercising in ancient Rome.

XANADU

Xanadu was a palace in Mongolia. It belonged to the fifth emperor of the Yuan dynasty, Kublai Khan, who ruled from the years 1260 to 1294. Five hundred years later Samuel Taylor Coleridge wrote about Xanadu in his poem about the emperor. Because that poem became very popular, the word *Xanadu* is now used to describe all sorts of dreamy places.

YAHOO

[**yah**-hoo] · *noun*

A yahoo is someone who is loud and rude. Yahoo is also a word someone might shout if they're excited.

YAK

[**yak**] · *noun*

A yak is a type of ox that has long hair and lives in Tibet.

YEANLING

[**yeen**-ling] · *noun*

A yeanling is a young sheep or goat.

YEARN

[**yurn**] · *verb*

If someone yearns for something, they really want it, but they might never get it.

YEASAYER

[**yey**-sey-er] · *noun*

A yeasayer is someone who always has a positive attitude. A yeasayer might also be someone who has a hard time saying *no* to others.

YEPSEN

[**yep**-suhn] · *noun*

A yepsen is the bowl shape two hands make when they're cupped together. A yepsen is also the amount of something that can be held when the hands are in this position.

YESTERYEAR

[**yes**-ter-yeer] · *noun*

When someone uses the word yesteryear, they're talking about a time in the past, and they're usually talking about good memories from that time.

YETI

[**yet**-ee] · *noun*

The yeti is a legendary monster that lives in the Himalayan mountains.

YEX

[**yeks**] · *verb*

When someone yexes, they're either hiccupping or crying.

YODEL

[**yohd**-l] · *verb*

When someone yodels, they sing in a special way where they quickly go back and forth from lower notes to very high notes.

YOMP

[**yahmp**] · *verb*

If someone yomps, they go on a difficult hike while carrying heavy equipment.

YONDER

[**yon**-der] · *adjective*

Yonder is an old-fashioned way to say *over there*.

YORE

[**yohr**] · *noun*

If someone talks about the days of yore, they're talking about a period of time from long ago.

YURT

[**yoort**] · *noun*

A yurt is a type of circular tent traditionally used as a home for traveling groups of people in Central Asia.

YUZU

[**yoo**-zoo] · *noun*

A yuzu is a type of citrus fruit that's round and yellow and has a sour flavor.

YODEL

Yodeling is very popular in Switzerland, Austria, and other areas with a lot of mountains. This style of singing is used to help people communicate with each other. When you're high up on a mountain, you can hear people yodel from far away.

ZAATAR

[**zah**-tahr] · *noun*

Zaatar is a mixture of herbs and spices that's popular in Middle Eastern cooking.

ZEAL

[zeel] · *noun*

Zeal is a feeling of passion and excitement about something.

ZEDONK

[**zee**-dongk] · *noun*

A zedonk is an animal that is half zebra and half donkey.

ZEITGEIST

[**tsahyt**-gahyst] · *noun*

When people use the word zeitgeist, they are talking about the popular feelings and ideas of an era.

ZENOGRAPHY

[zee-**nog**-ruh-fee] · *noun*

Zenography is the study of the planet Jupiter.

ZEPHYR

[**zef**-er] · *noun*

A zephyr is a soft and pleasant breeze.

ZEPPELIN

[**zep**-lin] · *noun*

A zeppelin is a type of large airship that was popular in the early 20th century. Airships are flying machines that were used to take people and things from place to place before airplanes were common.

ZEST

[zest] · *noun*

If someone has zest for an activity or thing, they really enjoy it.

ZEUGMA

[**zoog**-muh] · *noun*

A zeugma is a type of play on words where one word is used in two different ways in relation to the other words in the sentence. For example: *She devoured her book and a sandwich.*

ZEUSAPHONE

[**zoos**-*uh*-fohn] · *noun*

A zeusaphone is a type of electronic musical instrument that releases electricity in the form of bolts of light and sound. Another name for the zeusaphone is the singing Tesla Coil.

ZONK

[zongk] · *verb*

If someone zonks out, they fall asleep very quickly and suddenly.

ZILCH

[zilch] · *noun*

Zilch is a casual way to say *nothing* or *zero*.

ZOOLOGIST

[zoo-**ol**-*uh*-jist] · *noun*

A zoologist is someone who studies animals.

ZOETROPE

[**zoh**-ee-trohp] · *noun*

A zoetrope is a hollow cylinder-shaped object with small slits around the outside and a series of images inside. When it spins, the images inside look like they're animated, like a cartoon.

ZYGODACTYL

[zahy-*guh*-**dak**-til] · *adjective*

If a bird is zygodactyl, its feet have two talons or toes facing forward and two facing backward.

ZEPPELIN

The first time a zeppelin flew through the air was in the year 1900. It was 420 feet long and had two propellers. It could go as fast as 20 miles per hour.

END NOTES

WHY ARE THERE ONLY DIFFICULT WORDS IN THIS DICTIONARY?

Usually when we think about dictionaries, we think about a resource that has any word we could ever possibly want to know the meaning of. However, that's not how dictionaries always were. The first dictionaries in English were dictionaries of difficult words, just like this book. They were often collections of vocabulary from very specific topics like gardening, law, medicine, and words borrowed from other languages. It's only in the last few hundred years that dictionaries have been thought of as general-purpose reference books.

Now that you've read this book from cover to cover, what is your favorite word? Has it changed since reading *The Dictionary of Difficult Words*?

Jane's favorite word is: **DEIPNOSOPHIST** (page 19)

Louise's favorite word is: **AILUROPHILE** (page 7)

THEY

Though it might seem like a very simple word, there's a lot of debate over *they*.
Some people don't like it when you use *they* when you're talking about one person.
Instead, they think you should use *he* or *she*. However, this can sometimes be a problem.

What if you don't know the gender of the person you're talking about?
What if a person asks you to use *they* when you're talking about them?

The good news is, it's perfectly fine to use *they* when you're talking about one person.
If we look at writing from a long time ago, we can see that the word
they has been used for at least 700 years to talk about one individual person.
This book has used *they* in this way, and you can too!

WHAT MAKES A WORD REAL?

Lexicographers don't decide when a word becomes real. You do! Anyone can make up
a word. All you have to do is start using it. If you use it, it's real.

Just because a word isn't in any dictionary doesn't mean it isn't a real word. Each time a new
word is added to a dictionary, it takes a lot of time and energy. Lexicographers wouldn't be
able to add all the words that exist to a dictionary even if they knew every single word.

So go forth into the world and be creative with language! Make up as many words as you
want. Your words might not ever make it into a dictionary, but they are still real.

To my favorite centenarian, Minnie Solomon.—J. S.

To Betty Lockhart, who loved words, especially crosswords.—L. L.

Brimming with creative inspiration, how-to projects, and useful information to enrich your everyday life, Quarto Knows is a favorite destination for those pursuing their interests and passions. Visit our site and dig deeper with our books into your area of interest: Quarto Creates, Quarto Cooks, Quarto Homes, Quarto Lives, Quarto Drives, Quarto Explores, Quarto Gifts, or Quarto Kids.

The Dictionary of Difficult Words © 2019 Quarto Publishing plc.
Text © 2019 Jane Solomon. Illustrations © 2019 Louise Lockhart.
Pronunciations provided by Dictionary.com, with modifications
made by Laura Patsko for UK pronunciations.
First published in 2019 by Frances Lincoln Children's Books,
an imprint of The Quarto Group.
400 First Avenue North, Suite 400, Minneapolis, MN 55401, USA.
T (612) 344-8100 F (612) 344-8692 www.QuartoKnows.com
The right of Jane Solomon to be identified as the author and Louise Lockhart
to be identified as the illustrator of this work has been asserted by them in
accordance with the Copyright, Designs and Patents Act, 1988 (United Kingdom).
A catalog record for this book is available from the British Library.
ISBN 978-1-78603-811-1
The illustrations were created in Photoshop and using a pen on the iPad.
Set in Louise Lockhart's handlettered type.
Published by Rachel Williams
Designed by Karissa Santos
Edited by Katy Flint
Production by Jenny Cundill

Manufactured in China CC112020
9 8 7 6